Read-About® Geography

Moscow

By Allan Fowler

Consultant
Linda Cornwell, Learning Resource Consultant,
Indiana Department of Education

Children's Press®
A Division of Grolier Publishing
New York   London   Hong Kong   Sydney
Danbury, Connecticut

Visit Children's Press® on the Internet at:
http://publishing.grolier.com

Designer: Herman Adler Design Group

Library of Congress Cataloging-in-Publication Data

Fowler, Allan.
    Moscow / by Allan Fowler.
      p. cm. — (Rookie read-about geography)
    Includes index.
    Summary: An introduction to Russia's capital city, its history, people,
and famous sights.
    ISBN 0-516-21558-2 (lib. bdg.)   0-516-26557-1 (pbk.)
    1. Moscow (Russia)—Juvenile literature. [1. Moscow (Russia)]
I. Titles. II. Series.
DK601.2.F69   1999   98-37341
947`.31—dc21   CIP
                                               AC

©1999 Children's Press®
A Division of Grolier Publishing Co., Inc.
All rights reserved. Published simultaneously in Canada.
Printed in the United States of America.
1 2 3 4 5 6 7 8 9 10 R 08 07 06 05 04 03 02 01 00 99

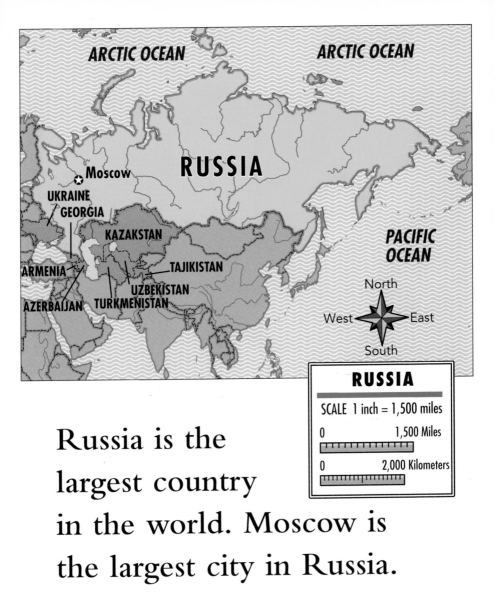

Russia is the
largest country
in the world. Moscow is
the largest city in Russia.

More than eight million
people live in Moscow.

Moscow is also Russia's
capital.

A capital is the home of
a country's government.

This is St. Basil's Cathedral in Moscow. (A cathedral is a large church.)

Look at all those towers! Each tower has an onion-shaped dome on top.

Each dome is painted in a different pattern and in different colors.

7

St. Basil's was built hundreds of years ago.

So were many other buildings in Moscow.

St. Basil's faces a big, open space called Red Square.

Long ago, the square was a marketplace. Now parades and ceremonies take place there.

A parade in Red Square

The Kremlin

The Kremlin stands next to Red Square. Brick walls surround the Kremlin.

Leaders of the country's government used to meet here.

Now they meet in another part of Moscow.

Some buildings in the
Kremlin are museums.
They used to be cathedrals
or palaces.

Moscow was born in
the Kremlin more than
800 years ago.

Then the city spread
out from the Kremlin.

The Moscow History Museum is inside the Kremlin.

16

Winters in Moscow are
very cold and long.

It snows about forty
days a year.

But people there have
a lot of fun in the winter.

People who live in
Moscow enjoy visiting
Gorki (GOR-kee) Park.

In winter, they can
ice skate at the park.

In summer, they can
ride in boats or play
tennis there.

Gorki Park

Russian hockey players

Moscow sports fans watch ice hockey in winter.

During summer, they
watch soccer games
at Dinamo Stadium.

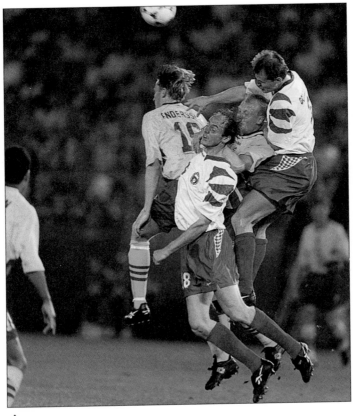

A soccer game

Ballets are danced and operas are sung at the Bolshoi (BOL-shoy) Theatre.

Dancers of the Bolshoi Theatre

Acrobats in the Moscow Circus

Clever bears, clowns, and acrobats perform at the Moscow Circus.

Moscow has an underground train system called the Metro.

The Metro stations are well known for their beauty. They are filled with works of art.

A Moscow Metro station

What would you eat if you went to Moscow? You could eat borscht (BORSHT), a soup made from beets.

A bowl of borscht

A Russian girl eating shashlik

Or try shashlik (shahsh-LEEK), meat cooked on a skewer.

Some of Moscow's buildings might remind you of home.

There are even a few McDonald's restaurants!

But you should visit Moscow to enjoy the many things that are different from home.

A McDonald's restaurant in Moscow

Words You Know

Kremlin

dome

cathedral

Red Square

30

acrobats

ballet

borscht

ice hockey

Metro

museum

shashlik

soccer

31

Index

About the Author

Allan Fowler is a freelance writer with a background in advertising.
Born in New York, he lives in Chicago now and enjoys traveling.

Photo Credits

Photographs ©: AllSport USA: 21, 31 bottom right (Jonathon Daniel); AP/Wide
World Photos: 20, 31 middle left (Tom Hanson); Envision: 26, 31 top right
(Steven Needham); Folio, Inc.: 16 (Cynthia Foster); Gamma-Liaison, Inc.: 4,
7, 30 right (Buck Kelly), cover , 8 (Vlastimir Shone); H. Armstrong Roberts,
Inc.: 15, 31 bottom left (B. Krubner); Monkmeyer Press: 27, 31 bottom center
(Ullmann); Panos Pictures: 29 (Gregory Wrona); Peter Arnold Inc.: 23, 31 top
left (Norman Benton), Sovfoto/Eastfoto: 11, 12, 19, 22, 25, 30 top left, 30
bottom left, 31 top center, 31 middle right (Tass).
Map by Joe LeMonnier.